Crickets Are Chirping *but*
No One Can Hear Them

When Loved Ones Develop Dementia and Loss of Hearing

Inge Logenburg Kyler

authorHOUSE®

AuthorHouse™
1663 Liberty Drive
Bloomington, IN 47403
www.authorhouse.com
Phone: 1 (800) 839-8640

Published by AuthorHouse 06/20/2017

ISBN: 978-1-5246-9673-3 (sc)
ISBN: 978-1-5246-9672-6 (e)

Library of Congress Control Number: 2017909530

Print information available on the last page.

PRELUDE

When my mother was in her late eighties, my sister and I realized we were suddenly faced with problems we didn't know how to handle. We both searched for books to read on what to do. We couldn't find the support we needed. I began keeping a journal and vowed to write my own story.

Watching parents have health problems while they age is a wrenching time. Decisions that must be made with them or for them is not easy. Some people manage to keep their parents at home and care for them, but that's not possible for everyone to do. Each person has to weigh the pros and cons of each decision.

It's not honors and certificates or degrees that make people famous or important. Rather, it's how a life is lived, how it is shared, and who that life touches. Mom touched a lot of lives. In our eyes, she was a great lady. May the story of her later years give encouragement to others who are faced with similar concerns. Most of all, we found that keeping a sense of humor throughout the crises we were all enduring, was important. It wasn't easy, especially when we saw the effects of Mom's declining health. But we tried.

This story would not have been possible without the loving care of Maplewood Home, Inc. staff under the leadership of Betty Breakey. Nor would it have been possible without the care of Mom's primary physician, Dr. Edward Ball, who was so patient and understanding. Nor would it have been possible without support of our own family members, such as my patient husband who helped throughout the many years of concern and care; and my loving sister and her husband, who shared with the care and love, as well. We did things together.

We may not have always agreed with each other in our decision-making, but we cooperated in a spirit of love that Mom would have appreciated. Also, our families need to be thanked for their understanding while we spent so much time with gramma and grandpa. We hope that when our time comes, someone will care about us as much as we cared about those two precious souls, Mom and Sam.

Wintering

It is a subtle thing, this wintering.
One day the fields are lush and green
and edged in hepatica along the fence row
with blossoms that sometimes are lost
to storm clouds and heavy rains.
But then we awaken one morning
to snow cresting on freshly plowed cornrows
and trees that tower stark and lonely
devoid of leaves, and we wonder,
what happened in between?
How did this transaction occur, and when?
We know only that migrating birds,
the cedar waxwing, the longspur, the sandhill crane
visit but momentarily as they rest
and swoop over our dwelling on their journey south
to leave us standing in the doorway watching,
an ache in our hearts and a longing in our souls.
We suddenly feel very alone.
We are suddenly like those migrating birds,
here for a summer, and then
it is fall and we must move on.
We store memories away like dried roses
to reflect upon.
Leaves bloom and fall. Doors open and close
and another chapter in our life is finished.

CHAPTER 1

It was 11 a.m. before I got through on the telephone. "Mom," I asked, "would you like to come over today?" My sister and I had mother on alternate weekends. This was my weekend.

"No," Mom said. "It's too cold to go out." Well then, I thought, perhaps we could have a tea party at her place. I heated a pot full of tea and poured it carefully in the big thermos and packed two small teacups with saucers, a spoon and napkins, along with a little cloth, into a satchel.

Earlier in the day I had baked some spice cupcakes. I selected half a dozen and placed them in a tin, grabbed my crewel needlework, and decided I was ready to go. I was prepared to spend the whole afternoon if she wanted me to.

"Your mother really misses you girls," said Frances, the bedridden resident in Room 1, and I felt a tinge of guilt because I came only every other weekend. Since I worked during the day and often had to attend meetings in the evening, as well, every other weekend was the best I could do. If I lived far away, I reasoned, I would not even be able to visit that often.

I found a small snack tray, spread out my goodies, and we had our tea party. Mom loved it. I didn't talk a lot as Mom was hard of hearing and mixed up almost everything I said, which meant I had to practically yell my conversation.

My sister and I had discussed getting Mom a hearing aid, but with her record for losing things, and having difficulty adjusting to new things, we decided a hearing aid might just add to her stress.

It was a subtle change, what happened to Mom. We would drive the one and a half-hour distance to visit her and when we arrived, noticed that she was getting quite forgetful. She kept two kitchens in her 1930's style little ranch home. The main kitchen was on the first floor. It was a small room with windows above the sink. The windows were so high she couldn't reach to open or close them. The window coverings were polka dot panels. I don't know how she got the curtains up there unless she stood on a chair. I shuddered at the thought!

The kitchen had a small stove with burners but no oven. There just wasn't room. The cupboards were placed high, making it awkward for her to reach and much more impossible for her to clean. For that reason we spent a lot of time trying to help her take care of them. There was only room for a small table, several chairs, and a refrigerator.

There was a dining area in the living room. That's where she kept her "good" table, chairs and hutch. The bathroom was small but adequate. The three bedrooms seemed to serve her needs and Sam's.

Mom had married Sam shortly before she retired from her job at the State. She had been alone for a few years after my Dad died and was lonely. She didn't like being without a man. When she decided she wanted to date, she contacted a dating agency with the result that men came from all over the state to woo and court her.

We were happy to see Mom enjoying life, but we were more than a little concerned with the character of the men that came to call. But we kept quiet. We didn't want to interfere. Probably if we had, she wouldn't have had the brief unhappy relationship she had before she met and married Sam. But then, maybe it would have happened anyway.

She had married Don. He seemed like a caring individual, but we found out after the fact, that he had a problem. Actually, he had more than one problem. Kind and gentle though he was, he wasn't dealing with a full keg of brains. We felt sorry for his Mom and Dad who we genuinely liked, but Don proved incapable of doing anything, whether in the kitchen or in the bedroom. Mom was heartbroken. She kept it to herself for quite a while, and then consulted an attorney and had the marriage annulled. This happened only after an episode when Don nearly burned down the house when he was trying to cook something in the kitchen. Enough was enough. Mom wanted a husband who would be a helpmate and lover. Being a substitute caretaker was not her idea of a marriage.

She met Sam at a dance, and they were soon a steady twosome. When they married, the family gathered together and wished them joy and blessings. It was good to see Mom happy. I sewed myself a cranberry wool dress to wear to her wedding. A reception was held in her cozy basement in her house in town.

While my sister and I were busy raising our families, we always took time to visit with Mom and sit down and have a cup of tea or listen to her play the piano. She had always played the piano, for as long as I can remember. She never cared much for television or radio. Of course television was something that didn't become available to us until in the mid fifties, so it hadn't become a habit. The piano was her life. When she was fifty, she started taking formal lessons and soon graduated to giving lessons to children in the neighborhood.

Our children received their instructions where to locate "Middle C", and how to properly hold their hands at the keyboard as soon as they could reach the piano. I never had much interest in the piano. I had other interests, and when I did sit down to play, Mom was so critical of my timing and hand placement that I decided it was easier to forget the whole thing.

After Mom married, she decided to sell the house and move to another town that was a good hour or so away. She and Sam wanted to be alone, we gathered, plus she wanted to be closer to her cousins of which she was very fond. We hated to see them move away. After they left, we would drive by the house and see other people in the windows and we felt sad.

But, we reasoned, Mom was happy, and that was what counted. She and Sam moved several times after they left our area. One time they moved into a trailer. We were horrified to discover that Sam was using the kitchen area for his workshop. His power tools were going full blast and sawdust was all over the place. But Mom didn't seem to mind. As long as no one interfered with her playing the piano, she was content.

When they moved into their last little house, Mom was quite taken with the older neighborhood. She liked to be around people she could visit. It was a well-built brick house, but quite dated in the interior. No matter. Mom liked it, and it was her house.

To make up for the small kitchen, Mom did most of her cooking in the basement on a little gas stove. As the years went by, we noticed that both kitchens needed a lot of cleaning up. Flour and sugar were everywhere. Mom liked to bake cookies, breads, and German kuchen. She didn't like us in the kitchen cleaning up after her. We tried to do it diplomatically.

3

We insisted that she play the piano, so some of us could retreat to the kitchens for major clean up while we listened to the piano music drifting through the house.

But the kitchens were getting worse. Grease started accumulating faster than we could keep it cleaned. Pots and pans of various sizes and shapes were everywhere. All of them needed to be washed. We made more trips on weekends, trying to keep the kitchen areas cleaned up as much as possible. Ants and mice were starting to have field days. They could find quite a lot of stuff to keep them nourished. We would clean things up, drive home, worry, and then go back another weekend and clean up all over again.

When I lived at home in my childhood days, Mom was an immaculate housekeeper. How she did it all, I don't know. But I would come home from school to find her straddling chairs in the living room while holding wallpaper in one hand and cutting around ceiling light fixtures with the other. A big tub of wallpaper paste was on the floor. She wallpapered walls and ceilings, alike. Our coal furnace necessitated a thorough cleaning of the house each and every spring.

Mom would be painting the kitchen or sewing new curtains, and spent a lot of time peddling away on the treadle machine, sewing rag rugs for every room in the house. She baked bread, fried donuts, milked the cow, fed the chickens, staked the cow out in the field and strained and skimmed the milk. Mom was never very big and was really very thin. No wonder! For relaxation she sat down and played the piano. I don't recall ever seeing her take a nap or goofing off in any way. I don't think she had time to pick up a book. If she had any time at all, it was spent at the piano.

But now, Mom was getting a little wobbly and unsteady. We caught Mom going up the basement stairs on her knees while balancing hot dishes in her hands. This was not good! We tried planting the seeds for a move back to our area. Mom was immovable.

CHAPTER 2

Sam was starting to have physical problems. Doctor visits and hospital visits were becoming frequent. Then we received a call that Mom had a mini-stroke. She had been shopping in a local mall when someone found her outside with a loaf of bread in her hands and she didn't know where she was or where she had parked the car. We were getting really concerned now.

Meanwhile, the cousins of which she was so fond were aging and dying off. Soon, they were all gone and there was no reason for Mom and Sam to be so far away from us. We were afraid she would get scalded carrying hot dishes up and down the stairs. She might have another stroke, and what would we do? We worked on the "move." Finally, she agreed to put the house up for sale. Like a lot of houses, it took time. Buyers would come and look and not return.

Mom was quite happy about it all. If no one comes to buy the house, she reasoned, then she wouldn't have to move. She loved her little house. She loved the proximity of a little park where she would go and read in the summer afternoons. She had a neighbor she really liked.

But there was one neighbor that gave her nothing but trouble. Mom complained to the police but they said there was nothing they could do. It was a young couple that lived beside her. They did everything they could do, to torment this older couple. They turned their garden hose on Mom's clothes that hung on the lines in her back yard. They threw dog dirt over the fence. They blasted the radio outside Mom's bedroom so she couldn't sleep at night. It was awful! It seemed there was nothing to be done about the situation.

We worried, and stewed, and prayed. Mom's little cat disappeared. Foul play had befallen it, we thought. Finally, a serious buyer appeared on the scene. A move was eminent! All of us went into full gear to make preparations. We had decided to move Mom and Sam to an apartment closer to us. But we had to dispose of a lot of stuff first.

There was a LOT of stuff! Sam liked to attend flea markets. This was fine, except he brought most of it home. The garage was so full of junk they couldn't put their car in. Finally, a junk dealer was contacted to come and haul the junk away. I don't remember how many loads it took until it was finally emptied.

We started emptying the small shed out back. A buyer was coming to get it. When we got it ready for the move, we found the flattened dehydrated remains of Mom's little cat. Poisoned, we thought, probably from the nasty neighbor. We never told Mom about our find. We just delicately dumped the cat in the trashcan. It had probably been under there a year, at least, and not much was left but hair. It was definitely little Penelope.

The closing of the house came before we got everything packed. Mom hired movers. The movers diligently packed everything including trash, empty boxes, junk, and whatever they saw. We found it all when the moving van arrived at her apartment.

We hurried to the apartment before she got there. Mom was still driving in those days. Sam was not allowed to drive anymore because of his eyes. However, we knew he still did, from time to time. "I just follow the white lines," he said, and we cringed at the thought.

In downtown Detroit, where Mom had to go for doctor appointments for herself and Sam, the only way she could get into the main traffic on main streets was to "lay on the gas pedal and horn at the same time" and drive out of the driveway. We wonder how many heart attacks she caused by doing that!

On moving day Mom drove in ahead of the moving van. We were at the apartment waiting to welcome her. We helped with the placement of the furniture. All of this couldn't have happened too soon, we realized as we unpacked boxes of junk and carried box full after box full of junk to the dumpster. We opened dresser drawers and dollar bills spilled out. At least the movers were honest, and if they had taken a few, we wouldn't have known anyway.

We were quite exhausted from all of this, needless to say, but we were happy that we had both of them closer to us. But our problems were far from over. Mom and Sam never could figure out the thermostat in their apartment. They would turn on the air when they were freezing and the heat when they were roasting. They just couldn't get it.

The refrigerator and stove presented problems, too. We found remains of melted plastic in the oven from food dishes that were never meant to be baked. The content of mold and mildew in the refrigerator was enough to wipe out a town, we worried, but even then, Mom didn't like us "cleaning out" her things. "Play us a song, Mom," we would say, and while she played the piano, we feverishly sweated in the kitchen, discarding the green lunchmeat from the refrigerator and scraping melted plastic off the oven.

All of this was not done without guilt. We wanted to visit with Mom and Sam, and not have to always be busy cleaning up after them. They wanted us to visit, too, so it was a delicate situation. We stopped to see them every day after work, to find out how they were doing. One day the toilet was plugged, and the landlord was not available. My husband took it apart, and, lo, a pair of false teeth fell out!

"No," said Sam, "they aren't mine!" They weren't Mom's either. Sam was always losing his hearing aid. Most of the time we think he did it on purpose. Mom would nag at him about something or other, and he would take out his hearing aid so he couldn't hear her. We would spend time searching under the couch, the bed, the piano, under pillows, etc., until finally we found it.

Sometimes we had the same problem with false teeth. Sam didn't know where they were, and we would search all over the house until we found them. Sometimes they were in a coat pocket. Sometimes they were under the kitchen table.

"Mom," we said, as we were totally exhausted by this time, "you need help. How about if we hire someone to come in and clean for you?" But Mom was insistent she didn't want anyone "meddling" in her apartment, including us. We went ahead and hired someone anyway, but no matter whom we hired, and what our instructions were, they either would fail to show up or Mom would fire them as soon as they came in the door.

We would bring Mom and Sam over to our house as often as we could. Sam loved to sit on the back deck. Mom loved to play the piano. One evening I said to Sam, "Just listen to those crickets." "What crickets?" Sam said. I realized he couldn't hear them. His hearing was so bad, even with the hearing aid in place, that he couldn't hear the noisy little creatures that were buzzing so loud in our back yard. The crickets were chirping but no one could hear them. Neither Sam nor Mom could hear the outside meadow noises of the seasons.

Sam loved playing the lottery. We found bag after bag stuffed with lottery tickets. He was waiting to cash in on the "big" one. We also noticed that Mom was sending out a lot of checks to charitable, and not so charitable, organizations. Mom and Sam both liked receiving mail. If I found letters asking for money, I threw them out when no one was looking. Mom sent money out to anyone who asked for it.

Sam couldn't see to read even with heavy glasses and magnifiers. He couldn't hear worth a darn and there just wasn't anything for him to do. We kept an eye on the lottery business and shook our heads, but it seemed a harmless activity and at least it kept him busy. We wished they would move to a retirement center with all its activities, but they weren't interested.

One cold November afternoon when we stopped by after work, Mom was standing in her walkway, crying. She was trying to carry a heavy basket of laundry from the laundry center. "Sam won't help," she wailed. We took the basket and got her into the house. From then on we took turns taking laundry home so she wouldn't have to carry it. But she resented that. She didn't like us meddling with her laundry.

Trips to the doctor and hospital were increasing for Sam. We could see that he was going downhill fast. They had both celebrated their 87th birthdays. The clock was ticking away.

CHAPTER 3

One Saturday in mid December I stopped over to help Mom with things. She was sitting on the sofa, crying away. "What's wrong, Mom?" I asked. "Oh," she said, her eyes red from crying. "I don't know who to give these things to or what to do!" Wrapping paper and packages surrounded her.

My Mom was a practical Mom. She had lived during the Great Depression. Because of that experience, when she bought us presents we knew they would be practical ones. Therefore it was not hard to decide who should get the kitchen broom, the box of aluminum foil, the clothespins, the brown work gloves or the flashlights. She especially liked flashlights. We didn't have electricity in our house until I was ten, so it was no wonder she felt a necessity for flashlights even today.

I wrapped everything up, labeled it all, and soothed her tears. "Whew," I thought, after the job was done. I went to the kitchen to tackle the mess in there.

A visiting nurse came, from time to time, to help take care of Sam's various problems. We always felt reassured when we knew she was coming. We knew Sam needed more care. "These two," she would admonish us, "need to be in a care home." But her words fell on deaf ears. There was no way Mom would consent to leaving her apartment.

Through all of this, they were in good spirits. Sam let me take him to the mall and put him in a wheelchair so he could shop for special presents. I loved taking him to the mall. I tried to talk Mom into going, too, but she would have none of it. She wouldn't be put in a wheelchair, she said, and would rather stay home and play the piano while the house was quiet. Her feet bothered her and she couldn't walk around in a big store anymore, but she would have no part of being in a wheelchair.

We knew Mom and Sam were having problems. Mom would complain that Sam's TV viewing, of which he was fond, was interfering with her piano playing. Sam liked TV, whereas Mom couldn't stand it. What else could he do? We found another TV and put it in his bedroom where he could retreat when Mom played the piano. That seemed to work.

But Mom was getting tired. She talked of divorce. "I am tired of taking care of a man," she would wail, and we would listen, reassure her, and go home. She was having trouble sleeping at nights and had started taking sleeping pills. It seemed to us that Mom was sleeping a lot during the day and that was why she couldn't sleep at night. But we weren't sure, as we were at work all day and didn't know exactly what was going on.

Mom and Sam still drove out to do their shopping and enjoyed going to the bank. They liked the convenience of a corner store even though the prices were higher. They liked to buy their own things. One time Mom was in a local bank while it was being robbed. She didn't know it until she went back in to get the cane she left standing by the counter. The door was barricaded when she tried to leave as the robber apparently was still inside.

Mom was unscathed and received a letter, later on, thanking her for her patience during the robbery and for her help in capturing the criminal. I don't know what help Mom was, as she didn't even know the bank was being robbed.

That was another thing we worried about. Mom and Sam would go to the bank and leave with dollar bills sticking out of their pockets! It's a wonder *they* weren't robbed!

When Mom decided she needed a new car, she went down to a local dealer while we were on vacation, bought a brand new fully loaded car, paid cash, and sold her old one for $500. When my coworkers found out about the paltry price that the dealership gave her for her old car, they went down and complained! But the deed was done.

We, as caretakers, were quite exhausted from watching over these two. Much as we loved them, it was beginning to take it's toll. "If you," said my boss, "don't put your folks in a home, you will end up in one!" We pondered those words. If only we could get Mom to go in a retirement home, but she wouldn't have it. The grandchildren got upset if we even mentioned it, and yet, THEY weren't the ones doing all the running, cleaning, supervising, and caring. They were observers from afar.

Mom was complaining more and more how difficult it was to take care of Sam. She was beginning to look more and more anxious and worn. We suspected she was into the sleeping pills big time. We looked over their pill supply and groaned. We tried to set up a system for them so they wouldn't get confused, but they couldn't even keep the days straight, let alone what pill to take or not to take. No matter what we tried, nothing seemed to work.

We suggested meals on wheels, among other things, but all our words fell on deaf ears. We knew events were mounting to a climax, but we could not foresee exactly what. It's a good thing!

CHAPTER 4

It was the car, all in all, that did Mom in. It was late evening when we got the call. Apparently Mom had an accident after leaving the beauty parlor. Her car was left in the parking lot while someone had given her a ride back to the apartment. It sounded like she was all right, and since it was Christmas Eve, there wasn't much we could do about the car until after the weekend. Did she want us to come over? No, she would be all right until tomorrow.

On Christmas Day we drove to Mom's apartment and brought her and Sam over to our house. Physically, Mom seemed to be all right, but she was obviously distraught. We weren't sure what had happened, whether she had fallen, had an accident or what. She didn't seem to be able to tell us. Meanwhile, our family joined us for Christmas dinner.

That's when the whole world fell apart! We had finished dinner when we realized that Mom obviously was not feeling well. I helped her to my bed in the master first floor bedroom and covered her with a blanket.

As the day wore on, Mom seemed more and more lethargic. She couldn't be stirred. When she asked to go to the bathroom, we had to carry her. Getting quite concerned, I called the family doctor. "Should I take her to the hospital?" I asked. "No," he said, "they will only run all kinds of needless tests and send her back home. Just let her rest and we'll see how she is during the next couple of days."

Full of doubt, I finished with the Christmas festivities and put things away. It was obvious Mom couldn't be moved. Tomorrow was a workday for all of us, but it didn't look like I would be able to go. My sister was on vacation in Florida, so it was up to my husband and I to take care of things. After discussion we decided that since Mom needed help to get to the bathroom, my husband would stay at the house with her. Meanwhile, I took Sam over to the apartment and stayed there with him.

Our spare bedrooms were upstairs via steep tiny stairs that are in all older farmhouses. There was no way that Sam could make it up those stairs. The weather outdoors was cold and snowy. I drove Sam to the apartment and tucked him in bed while I slept in Mom's bed in the next room.

The next day, Mom was immobile. She didn't seem to be coherent. Neither my husband nor I went to work. As the day progressed, Mom seemed to be in a sick stupor. At the apartment, I noticed that Sam was having problems, too. Even though we had been checking on both of them every day and had tried to keep the place neat and tidy, things were not right. For instance, buckets of clothes were soaking in the bathtub. I didn't want to think about what that might mean.

From what I could see throughout the apartment, both of these dear-loving souls, were having physical problems they couldn't contend with anymore. They had been trying to handle things that were just beyond their control.

The next couple of days were spent in my running back and forth between our own house and Mom's apartment. Our neighbor realized what was going on and suggested we take them both to the foster care home where she worked. "They have a couple vacant rooms now," she said. I called my sister who was vacationing in Florida and asked what do we do? We agreed that taking Mom to the Home seemed to be the smart decision. Worn and exhausted, we called the Home and made the necessary arrangements. We had both been aware for some time that things were not going right for Mom and Sam.

Mom seemed oblivious to her surroundings. As we drove her to the Home, she cheerily said, "Are we going through a hurricane?" The wind was blowing, and snow was piling up everywhere. It was quite a blizzard! We told Mom we were taking her to a place where people could care for her better than we could. She seemed totally unaware what was happening. We tucked her into a cozy room and went back to check on Sam. We couldn't leave Sam alone at the apartment. Months ago we had been told that he should be in a nursing home.

By now I had requested leave from my job under the Family Medical Act, but I knew that with the holidays over, I would have to return to work soon. We decided to take Sam to the same Home where Mom was staying. Back at their apartment, I helped Sam dress and told him we were going to the Home to see Mom. He was so hard of hearing, I don't know if he knew what I was saying, but he went along with it all. It was a terribly cold evening. In my distraught state, I suddenly realized I hadn't a clue where I was! The road did not look familiar at all. In my anxiety, somehow I had taken a wrong turn. "Oh no," I thought, "I'm lost on a cold, snowy evening with an old man who needs care, and I haven't a clue where I am!" But I calmed myself and realized that if I kept on driving, I would surely come to a road that would take me around to where I needed to go. It was an experience I will never forget!

I helped Sam through the door and got him situated in a room next to Mom's. After a few days at the Home, Mom rallied somewhat. "Why is Sam here with me?" she asked distraught. "I thought he was going to a nursing home." We didn't know what to say, but tried to calm her the best we could. Meanwhile, the Home let us know that Sam needed nursing home care. He was beyond the care of a foster care home. "It is too much," they said. "We can't do it."

Through all of this, I was in contact with my sister. A year earlier, she had accompanied Mom and Sam to visit his son in California. We remembered that he had said that "should father need the care of a nursing home I want him to live with me." We wondered if he really meant it. We had to do something. The foster care home could not care for him. Mom was not ready for a nursing home. We hated to separate them and knew their finances could not handle both of them being in separate facilities. What should we do?

We talked to Mom about Sam. She seemed to understand, and yes, he seemed willing to go to California, "if they wanted him." A call was placed. "Yes," the son said, "we will take Dad." I called the airport and arranged a flight. Then I started packing. As I looked through Sam's closet, I noticed that some of his pants were tacked with drapery hooks. Well, that was ingenious, I thought. Much of the clothing needed to be washed. I packed what clean clothes I could find, and piled up others for washing.

"Where is the little black car?" Sam asked as he sat on the edge of his bed watching me pack. I remembered seeing a broken car that I had tossed in the trash with a mountain of unmatched socks and torn underwear. I immediately felt guilty. I told him I would keep looking for it. A big lamp without a shade stood in the closet. "I was going to get a shade for it," Sam said. I tried to keep down the lumps in my throat.

It was a restless night. I woke several times to check on Sam. Plastic bottles full of urine were on the sink. It was too much! It seemed like I was in a nightmare world. Mom and Sam had said their good-byes the night before. A second trip had been made back to the Home when it was discovered that Sam had left his teeth there.

We tried to explain that he was going to California. He seemed to accept it. It would be better for him, we told him, as he could never get warm in Michigan. His tall lean skinny frame was always huddled in flannel shirts and sweaters, and he shivered all the time.

At four in the morning, the limousine arrived to take us on the two-hour drive to the Detroit airport. "You are lucky to be going now," said the driver, and went on to say "four inches of snow is expected later today." We sat quietly and thoughtfully. Tears were streaming down my cheeks. A wheelchair was waiting for us at the airport door. In just a matter of minutes, Sam was rolling down the runway away from us. I could not control my tears. It all seemed so unfair, and yet I knew Sam would receive care that he wouldn't receive if he remained in Michigan. His family wanted him and was eager to share his last years with him.

CHAPTER 5

It didn't seem that we could actually do such a thing—send Sam so far away. And yet we knew we had to do it. His family was grateful. We washed the rest of his decent clothes and sent them off. I packed papers and pictures, and anything that meant a lot to him, and we sent it off. We found some savings bonds and sent them along, too. We knew we would have to get into financial matters and divide some of Mom's money, and yet we didn't know how much she would need for her care at the Home. We didn't know what might lie ahead. We made an appointment with an attorney for guidance on what to do.

When I went back to work, I was so distraught, that I contacted our work counseling service and set up some sessions. I started keeping a journal. I prayed a lot. How could we possibly get through all of this?

Did Mom really need to be in a Home? We asked ourselves that question and made arrangements to have her tested at a local geriatric hospital. Mom, of course, objected. She didn't need any tests, she insisted, but we took her anyway. After a battery of tests, we were called in for a family conference.

"Did Mom have a stroke?" I asked, after all the other questions had been asked. "No," said the doctor looking directly at Mom. "She had a sleeping pill overdose." I remembered how Mom was always popping those pills. They were "little," she had said, so she must have felt she needed more than one. "Cookies and milk," the doctor said, "is what you need, not sleeping pills."

We couldn't believe this news. The doctor asked Mom how long she had been in the Home. "Oh, a year now," she said. "They take good care of me. I like it there." By this time, Mom had only been there a month or so. The evaluation revealed what we had known for a while. "Your mother needs direct supervision," repeated the doctors. They talked about dementia and we wondered what that meant and what to do.

Should we close out the apartment? We were still paying rent on it as well as the monthly rent at the Home. We knew we could not continue to do both. But we also knew that there was no way that Mom could be alone in the apartment. Nor was there any way she was in a mental or physical state to make any decisions regarding disposal of anything. We started packing again.

We decided to close out the apartment and move all of Mom's belongings to our pole barn. Fortunately, it was a big pole barn. The move began. At one point my sister announced the move was off! She wanted to bring Mom back to the apartment.

"What?" I asked. "You weren't here when she got ill. We've been going through hell. There is no way Mom can stay here." We had some tearful times. This was not easy. My sister had been especially close to Mom. It was hard for her to realize that now we had to be caretakers and take care of Mom instead of the other way around. The tables had turned, like it or not.

That is a wrenching realization, realizing that the one you love so dearly, and who has always taken care of you, suddenly can do it no longer. All of us sought counseling and read whatever we could about this dementia that was robbing us of our mother. We sorted, discarded, packed, and cried. Probably we cried more than anything else. Again, none of this seemed fair. But what else could we do?

We were worn out and distressed from all of this. Mom would call one day and plead for me to take her back home. "She doesn't want to talk to you," said my sister, and I felt a deep sense of guilt. But after awhile, Mom adjusted. Her cheeks became rosy again. We brought her over to our homes where she played the piano. She indicated an interest in taking guitar lessons.

I bought a small guitar and arranged for music lessons for the both of us. She would take guitar and I would take mandolin lessons. I didn't know if Mom could remember her assignments, and she couldn't, but it didn't matter. It was something she looked forward to. By then Mom was 88. I would dash out of the office, my mandolin in my hand, drive over to get Mom from the Home, and then drive us both back into town for our lessons every Tuesday.

Mom had her lesson first, and then would sit and listen while I had mine. I don't know if either one of us learned anything, but somehow that didn't matter. I was getting her out and we were both doing something different. It was a good diversion.

Mom didn't always want to come to our homes. "I'm busy today," she would say. "I have letters to write." We had moved Mom's piano to my sister's house. It seemed a reasonable thing to do. My sister's piano was an old upright. It needed to be replaced. I had a piano in my own house and was happy with it, even though it, too, was old. The home had a piano and an organ. "No," Mom had insisted, "I don't want my piano here. It's fine where it is." But she worried about it. "Don't keep the piano keyboard closed," she would say, "or moisture will build up and ruin it." Nor did she want little kids banging on it.

The workers at the Home were thoughtful and caring. We felt very fortunate to have our mother in the care of loving caretakers. It was a small Home, housing ten to twelve adults. Men and women stayed there. Mother liked the men. In fact, she became fond of several, as time went by. It seemed amusing and harmless. There are some things the body does not forget. But the men who came, didn't live long. They died just as Mom was getting attached to them.

Mom's life savings were being poured into the Home, but we were glad that she had those resources. An insurance policy she had for home care refused to help with anything. We didn't know how long Mom would have to stay in the Home or if eventually she would need to be in a nursing home. The world was full of unknowns so we took a day at a time.

Not all families have the resources for such care. Some families manage to keep their loved ones at home. That is to be esteemed but is not possible for everyone. Mom liked to be around people, and liked visiting with the others at the Home. There were activities and good food. She no longer had to cook or clean or do laundry. She seemed happy. She would not have been happy cooped up in a little apartment or being home alone while I was at work.

Mom went for walks in the back yard at the Home. A chair was placed by the far fence row where she could sit and read. This was quite a distance from the house. Sometimes she washed out underwear and hung it in tree branches by the chair. It probably reminded her of the days she hung up the wash when we lived in the Pennsylvania mountains.

One time, her chair tipped over and she fell into a patch of poison ivy! We had to take her to the doctor for treatment. At least she didn't suffer any broken bones. The ivy was sprayed and eradicated. When Mom told us about the incident, she said, "Oh, I boohooed back to the house and they put a hot compress on my forehead."

Mom liked to watch the farmers cutting their hay. She wanted to see cows.

"Where are the cows?" she would ask. We had a cow when we lived in Pennsylvania. She wanted to see some today. I would take her for drives in the country and we would go looking for cows. I would stop the car so she could watch them. She liked horses, too, and pigs. But she preferred cows.

CHAPTER 6

When we told family members and friends that Mom was in a Foster Care Home due to dementia, some of them did not understand. It was hard for us to understand, also. Exactly what was dementia?

I poured over books in the library and the Internet on my home computer. But in those years, there was not much information to be found. No one, it seemed, fully understood dementia. Years later, in further research, we established that dementia may be caused by Alzheimer's disease, but it could also be caused by a variety of other illnesses, an accident, or neurological disorders.

I rationalized dementia with arthritis. There is arthritis, and then there is rheumatoid arthritis. In other words, there are many forms of arthritis. They are not all and one the same.

Mother had had a series of mini strokes. It is possible that her dementia was a result of them. I read that dementia meant memory loss. Persons with dementia need direct supervision. That was certainly the rule in Mom's case. In years past it was probably referred to as senility or just "old age."

Today we are more informed about the various diseases that affect the elderly. There has been more research with the result that answers can be found quickly by just searching on the Internet. Our doctors and medical personnel are more informed. There are many more sources of help today than there were when Mom was diagnosed.

It was a difficult time especially since many people let us know that they would "never think of putting there loved ones in a nursing home." To those persons I respond by stating that everyone has to make his or her own decisions. Mom was happy in the Home. She would not have been happy living with us. She liked people and wanted to be surrounded by them.

We were fortunate that Mom had enough money, due to her very frugal life style, that she could "pay her way."

If that had not been the case, I am not sure what we would have done. Probably she would have gone into a nursing home, or maybe we would have worked it out somehow that she could have stayed with us.

But to have home care, there has to be available home care workers to assist. When we searched for workers, we were unable to find reliable ones in our area. The ones we did find, were so costly that there was no way we could afford them.

Mother had had a long-term health insurance, but it didn't cover this type of care. It covered only nursing home care. Therefore it was useless.

There are nice nursing homes. We have seen some terrible ones and some very clean ones. But we didn't want Mom in an institutional setting. Foster care homes seemed more personal and cozy. We also wanted her to have her own private room. Some people, however, do not like to have private rooms. My husband's mother was in a nursing home and was happy that she had a roommate in the adjacent bed.

We have to be sensitive to the needs and desires of our loved ones. But in that process it can be very wrenching for us. I was torn daily, by all the decisions. I cried until I couldn't cry any more. "Why was this happening?" I asked myself. It didn't seem fair. I had lost the Mom I knew.

In the end, it was the acceptance of it all. There was nothing we could do. My sister and I stayed on call for potential problems. We faithfully took Mom to the doctor, to the hospital, to the dentist, to the eye doctor, and all the places in which she needed medical attention.

We strained and pushed and pulled wheelchairs, prodded walkers, joked about the little funny habits Mom had, and, all in all, took everything one day at a time.

We each had families that needed attention. We needed attention ourselves, as well, and needed to get away. We made sure someone was available while the other one went out of town.

We sorrowed that friends and family did not take the time to visit Mom. We tried to understand. Yes, it is a busy world, and everyone is busy taking care of his or her own lives, but Mom missed everyone. She would ask about different friends and family even though she didn't recognize those who did come. I took photographs with me when we visited and we went over them again and again.

"This," I would tell Mom, "is your great-great-granddaughter." "What?" she would say, "Great great-granddaughter?" "Yes," I would say, and then proceeded to give her all the details. It wasn't easy, as I had to repeat everything a hundred times, but I felt she retained at least some of it.

But the hardest thing to accept was the condemnation we received from family in Germany. They could not understand why Mom was in a Home. "We take care of our elderly," they said in their letters. We were taking care of Mom, too, but in a different way.

People who kept their parents at home would look at us in disgust. That was hard to take. I got tired trying to explain to everyone, and after awhile, I just avoided some of them. I didn't need to explain, I decided. We were doing what we felt was best, and that was all that was important. Mom was happy and well cared for. That was all that mattered.

CHAPTER 7

We moved some of Mom's furniture into her room and made it cozy. I made new slipcovers for one of her old chairs as she did not want a new one. She certainly had enough money for new things but she didn't want them. Nor did she want a telephone, radio or, heaven forbid, television. She liked to read, write letters, and go out in the sitting room to play the piano.

When Mom came over to our place, she played the piano and then would wander around outside. "Why don't you get rid of that awful building?" she asked, pointing to our big barn. That old barn was my husband's pride and joy. The insurance man had insulted it, too, right after we moved to our farm just a couple years ago. "Take it down," he said, "and I will reduce your insurance." "If you want my business," countered my husband, "you will insure the barn," and he did.

Mom thought we lived too far away from other people. "You don't have any neighbors," she would say, as she looked around at the fields of meadow and hay around us. I worried about her, wandering around, and made sure that she didn't get too close to our rooster. Mom's cane was bright and shiny. Our rooster hated bright shiny things and was known to take into them. If he was outside of the pen when Mom was outside, I watched both of them very carefully.

Our dog, Gus, didn't like Mom's cane, either. "Why do you have such a big dog," she would say as she nudged Gus with her cane. Gus was our blonde Labrador retriever. He stayed in the kitchen and never wandered beyond the threshold into the dining room. His bed was under the kitchen counter, and invariably, Mom would spot him there. After all he was so big that how could you miss him? She would poke at him with her cane. He just scrunched closer to the wall, while watching her with his big brown eyes.

We took turns taking Mom to church. She didn't care much about going shopping. I wanted to take her to the mall, but she didn't want to go. She managed to call a cab, and went to the annual State Employees Retirement Picnic one summer day! She talked about getting a cab and "going home." The home she meant was back in Pennsylvania. This was Michigan! We worried, but the Home kept a close eye on her.

Mother was still having a time sleeping, even though she asked for cookies and milk like the doctor suggested. "Some wine would help," she said, and we would supply her with a bottle of wine and a wine glass. She kept the wine bottle behind her chair. The Home knew she had it, but pretended they didn't notice. We tried to keep her supplied with cookies, too.

Sometimes she would argue with some of the residents. They would want the lights turned on and she would go around and turn them off. We would hear about these little disagreements from time to time.

CHAPTER 8

She liked the activities that took place in the Home. "They brought in this big Christmas tree," she said that next Christmas, "and wouldn't tell us who would decorate it. And then in burst all these children who suddenly decorated the tree and sang songs. We all sang songs together. What a day it was!" We found out that a Girl Scout troop had come in and entertained the residents, to their delight! We felt grateful for that and made a mental note to thank them.

"On Mondays," said Mom, "the Music Man comes. He plays instruments and we sing and play games." I never attended any of those activities. I was so busy at work, those days. It was all I could do to visit when there was time. There just wasn't enough time in the day for everything that needed to be done.

I visited other elderly people, besides my mother. A dear friend was in a nursing home and had just celebrated her 103rd birthday. "I didn't want to get this old," she sobbed as the lady in the next bed yelled, "Oh shut up, you Old Bag!" I felt depressed when I left. All those people, sitting there, lying there, just waiting to die. It just didn't seem right.

In the newspapers I read about neighbors being upset because a "foster care home" was "moving in," and yet, do they realize the importance of those homes? We don't know when and if we ourselves may need to go to one, and will there be room? Will they be available? I think people want those things out of sight so they don't have to think about them.

It's hard for family members to see a loved one go to a Home. The children didn't want to visit their gramma. "I want to remember her how she was," they would say, and yet she missed seeing them. I would take photographs of them and kept telling her stories about them, but they were busy with their own lives. It distressed them to see their gramma in a Home. I tried to understand.

The minister of the church Mom had faithfully attended never once came to visit her. The ladies of the church sent her cards, from time to time, but no one came to visit. I felt bad about that. Mom had written a lot of checks to the church, but no one would take the time to come out and visit her. We took her to church as often as we could, but after awhile, it was no longer possible for her to ascend the very steep steps to the entrance. I kept thinking someone from the church would come out to the Home, but they never did.

"I won't be around much longer," Mom would frequently say. She talked about the other residents. One was in her 90's. Mom thought that was awfully old, and yet Mom was almost that herself. Residents came, died and new ones moved in. No one, it seemed, was there very long.

At her annual exam the doctor asked if she was eating a good diet. "Oh yes," she said, "I get real good food!" All in all, Mom was staying healthy. She took no pills except one a day to prevent strokes. "I hope," said the doctor to my mother, "that I can be half as healthy as you are at your age."

Mom felt guilty about us having to drive her to the doctor and other places. "I didn't have this problem with my mother," she said. "But Mom," I said, "your mother died when she was only 65." "That's true," she said thoughtfully.

"I don't feel like company today," said Mom one day when I was visiting and she was lying on the bed. I took off my coat and went through her mail. It was old mail. Mom liked to keep old mail around in various boxes and containers. Some of the mail was twenty years old, but she still liked to look at it. "Don't throw that empty cracker box away," she said, as I began sorting and was in the process of discarding. "I might need it for something," she added, and rolled back over.

When we lived in Pennsylvania in the 40's and 50's, most mothers stayed at home. My father, along with a lot of other men, didn't like to have their wives work outside the home. They wanted to be the sole bread winners and were proud of it. I appreciated having Mom home when I got home from school, and felt sorry for some of my friends who had to go home to an empty house. When I went home Mom would be in the kitchen and there would be the aroma of donuts frying on the stove.

"My regret," said Mom one day when she was in the kitchen watching me wash dishes, "was that I didn't learn how to drive and go to work when we lived in Pennsylvania." "No mother," I told her, "that was not a bad thing. We enjoyed having you home. You were a good mother, always there for us." And it was true.

In those days we lived three miles from town. It may as well have been fifty miles, as everything was meadow and woods between town and us. We lived in a quiet little valley. A large farm stood on the main road across the meadow from our house. A few other farms were scattered here and there on the hills, but we were quite isolated. Today the whole valley is an industrial park, and Route 80 crosses over the hill that was just beside our house.

"I should have learned to drive earlier than I did," Mom went on. "Why?" I asked. "We couldn't afford a second car." "That's right," admitted Mom. "Your Dad had to leave early for the mines and didn't get home until late. I suppose it wouldn't have done me any good to learn to drive." My Dad worked in the coal mines. That was the direct result of the Big Depression. There weren't any other jobs available. The choices of employment for many years were the coal mines, brickyards and railroads.

We did a lot of visiting in those days. Mom and I walked over the hill and visited the neighbor ladies during the week. On weekends we drove out to visit aunts and uncles who lived in other towns, or some of them came and visited us. We were very busy with relatives. All in all, we were a very close family.

"I suppose you're right," said Mom, leaning on her cane. We had to keep an eye on that cane. It was always disappearing. Finally, we put a piece of orange tape on it, so we could find it easier. We nearly lost it for good the day we went into the music shop to pick out the guitar for Mom. She had set the cane down, and suddenly realized it wasn't there! "My cane," she said, "it's gone!" I looked up and all I could see were wooden necks of guitars and mandolins. We'll never find it, I thought, but suddenly someone yelled, "I found it!"

Even with orange tape, the cane would disappear from our sight. We had to retrieve it from the church, people's houses, our own homes, and stores. We would find it stuck in the oddest of places. We spent so much time hunting for that cane that we thought of installing a beeper on it. Finally we bought another one for just such emergencies.

We finally had to sell Mom's car. We kept it around, for a while, at my sister's. Mom would get in it, stomp on the gas, and drive it around the block. I think she terrified the whole neighborhood. But she wouldn't give it up.

"If I still had my car," she would say, "you wouldn't always have to come and get me. I could drive myself!" Or she would say, "I couldn't drive out to get you anything for Easter, so don't get me anything either." We didn't know what to do about the car. But the geriatric team of specialists at the hospital where Mom was tested, intervened, wrote a letter to the Secretary of State, and her license was revoked. We put the car up for sale and in a week, it was gone. We all breathed a deep sigh of relief!

CHAPTER 9

It was Sunday evening when I stopped over to visit Mom. She was sitting at the dinner table. Her eyes were red and swollen.

'You're here," she said. "Did you hear about the trouble?"

"What trouble, Mom?" I asked as I patted her hand.

"It's the bill," Mom said as she patted some bread in her mouth. "I don't know where my husband went, and he is supposed to pay the bill." I thought to myself that this was going to be a difficult visit. Mom was inconsolable.

"She's been like this all day," said one of the caretakers. "John is confused, too, and said he lost a pony." John was another resident. I was accustomed, by this time, to expect just about anything from the residents. I remembered one resident, who, soon after Mom was admitted, stated that he just got done "putting off fire crackers." Most of the residents, like Mom, were in their eighties. Their minds just couldn't keep up with today.

There were also some residents that didn't like Mom. I read some place that the classmates we don't like usually end up with us in a nursing home. In one instance, a resident who kept trying to trip Mom in the hall, and swore at her under her breath, was a lady who was convinced, and she could have been right, that her husband had had a crush on Mom in years gone by. A lot of men had crushes on Mom. She was that type of lady. Everyone liked her.

I think about the caretakers in elderly care home. They certainly deserve more than minimum wage. We pay schoolteachers to teach our children but we can't spare anything to support the burgeoning homes that house our elderly loved ones. That's not right. We subsidize schools and education, but we provide no assistance for the care homes or families who are trying to care for parents.

Truly, I felt like a sandwiched parent. I was getting closer to retirement and needed to save money for that day. But I was growing worried that Mom's money might run out and we would need to help her. We would do it, no matter what. But it didn't seem right. I tried not to worry about it. We were caught in-between our own adult children, some of whom were undergoing problems of their own, and now our parents. Such stressful times.

We hoped that Mom's savings would last as long as she did, but we weren't sure that would happen or not. We weren't concerned about receiving an inheritance. When parents save money, it's their money, and I don't believe children have a right to expect anything. They gave us life and support while we were growing up. Now it was our turn to support them. We just hoped that her money would last as long as she did. But if it didn't, well, we would have to bite the bullet if and when that happened.

People who lived through the Great Depression had a different set of rules to live by. Mom would never think of eating out someplace where the meal cost more than $5.00! Nor would she pay a lot of money for clothes. She was raised in a frugal environment and that stayed with her all her life. In fact, we realized, after going through her finances, that she never sent medical bills to insurance companies. She paid for everything with cash and check.

Mom never bought anything through credit cards. We did find an instance where she had purchased a television, as well as a warranty agreement and over the years paid much more than the television was worth, and it wasn't even working right. It took several letters and telephone calls to get the warranty agreements cancelled. Too many companies take advantage of the elderly.

But it seemed that there should be some means to assist the elderly for health care, either in their own homes or in foster care homes. We were told Mom's care would be provided for should she enter a nursing home. But we were also told that entrance to a nursing home would divest her of all of her savings. Somehow, that didn't seem quite fair, and it seemed that there should be some sort of subsidy for persons who needed assisted living care.

Even assistance with accessory housing would be of benefit, but not many areas will allow an accessory building on a building site along with a family home in a residential area. Home health care is prohibitive. When we were debating what to do before Mom went into the Home we discussed home health care. There was no way under the sun that we could afford it. Home health care would have exhausted Mom's savings in a couple of years. We didn't know how long she would need care, and we worried.

When Mom was at the Home and needed health care attention, we had to bundle her up and take her out. That didn't seem quite fair when she was ill. But health care personnel wouldn't come to the Home, not to foster care homes, at least. It seemed so cruel to wrap Mom in a wool coat and scarf and take her out in the windy cold when she needed to see a doctor, but we had to do it. I remembered when I was a little girl and the doctor came to our house in the country. It seems there should be doctors who could make house calls to the elderly.

My sister and I took Mom to the dentist for new dentures. "Ouch, awww, you are hurting me," she would protest. The dentist was quite relieved when we finally were done. "You are scaring away my other patients," he would say. Mom was like that. If you just touched her, she would wince and yell in pain.

"Are you coming today?" Mom asked over the telephone. I replied that I would be there around 2 o'clock. When I got there, Mom was sitting at the table. "I thought you weren't coming until later this afternoon," she said, and I scolded myself for not telling the caretaker when I was coming. Other times I would come and she would say, "Why are you here? Or what do you want?" If I came to take her somewhere, she would dawdle and slowly move through the building telling everyone goodbye. It reinforced the importance of patience. I was developing patience I never knew I had.

Those were things we had to deal with. Mom got all confused in time, days and years. "Who are you?" she asked once, when I walked in wearing sunglasses. I took them off. "I didn't recognize you in those dark things," Mom said. Mom hated black. If I wore black, she would complain. "Why are you always wearing black?" she asked. I replied that it was a professional color, and that I had a professional job and that I had to look professional. She didn't buy it.

Mom had a big window in her room. "I can see the moon really well," she would say. She did have a good view of the moon coming up. Once in awhile she would see deer, too, running past the window. Mom liked to see things like that. One time we were driving her back to her Home during a driving rainstorm when a large buck suddenly reared up in the middle of the road! It was quite a sight! It shook Mom up, and she talked about it a long time afterwards.

CHAPTER 10

"I need to go to the eye doctor," Mom said. "These new glasses don't work at all." Those were words we hated to hear, for the eye doctor had told us there was nothing that could be done for Mom's eyes. Mom loved to read, but now was limited in doing so. We suggested talking books, but she didn't want that. "I want to read," she said, and our hearts broke.

We tried reading to her, but she was getting so hard of hearing, that we had to yell every word several times. It just wasn't worth it. When we took Mom to the eye doctor, we took along the glasses that were in her dresser drawer. "Hmm," said the eye doctor, "none of these are your mother's prescriptions!" There was no way of knowing whose glasses she had. The residents would wander around and visit in each other's rooms. Who knows where Mom's glasses were? We had the doctor print Mom's name inside the new glasses. But the new glasses didn't do much good, anyway, and she ended up losing them.

Mom's hair was hard to keep under control. We took her out for haircuts, until it was too difficult to do so. The caretakers would try to wash and curl it, but Mom protested a lot. She didn't like anyone touching her hair. She was proud of the fact that it wasn't gray. Mom always looked young for her age. She still asked for ice cubes in the morning, so she could rub them on her face. "It keeps me young," she would say, and all of us were making a mental note to keep ice cubes in the refrigerator. She also hated baths and claimed the caretakers were "trying to kill" her!

"I wonder how your Dad found me?" she asked suddenly one day while I was combing her hair. Mom liked to talk about the old days. "I remember now," she went on, "your Dad was visiting the old German Lutheran Church. He had just come from Germany and arrived at the church from the trolley that ran beside the road across from the church. Your grandfather was directing a boys' orchestra of horn players, and I told your father that he had to wait in the hall until the music piece was done."

"He was so handsome," she went on. "All the girls and their mothers had their eyes on him. But I got him. Everyone else wanted to invite him to dinner, but, Mom said, "he came to our house."

"It's your birthday today, and I missed it," said Mom when I visited one January afternoon. "It's okay, Mom," I said. I would have liked to have gone on and told her about the celebration, but her hearing made much conversation difficult.

"I'll go to the store," Mom went on. "Would you like some buttons?" She knew I was always sewing something. "Yes, buttons would be fine." I knew she couldn't get to the store, but I humored her and she was happy.

"What color," she went on, "of buttons would you like?" "Pink," I said. "Oh yes," she said, "that would look good with your shirt." It didn't make sense, but then, not much did anymore.

"I could still go to your home today," mother said as I looked at my watch and wondered if I should start getting her ready to take out, "but," she went on, "my stomach hurts and I would have to lie down as soon as I got there." I decided the effort of dressing her, putting on her boots and tucking her in the car might be a bit much on this snowy day, but then she said, "and then again…" I wondered what to do.

"It's not easy," I told my daughter over the phone, "dealing with parents when you are the caretaker." "Well, Mom," said my daughter, "write everything down so I will know how to take care of you when it's your turn!" I thought to myself that I wasn't ready to go anywhere just yet. But then, maybe we never are.

"They have to agree. You can't force them to sign anything," we were told when we wondered how to best handle Mom's financial matters. "I'm not signing anything," Mom had said. But in time she did consent to signing papers so both my sister and I could have power of attorney to handle her affairs. She also signed durable health papers. While we had the papers drawn up, we had papers drawn up for ourselves as well. One never knows. Mom had indicated she never wanted to be on life support. We respected her wishes.

We had a time, however, getting her to agree to direct deposit for her social security. She liked receiving her check and stuffing it in a drawer. This was not good. The Home didn't like money matters coming there, but after awhile, Mom agreed to sign direct deposit papers.

CHAPTER 11

"Do you know anything new?" asked Mom in a hopeful mood. I tried to think what I could tell her. I told her of the usual mundane news. "Anything new with you? I asked. "Oh yes," she said excitedly. "Frances fell and broke her hip! Poor Frances. We liked to visit. She lost her husband awhile back. Well, I guess we both lost our husbands," and she started getting teary eyed.

I noticed that Mom needed to have something done, again, with her hair. "I'll make an appointment for you at the beauty shop," I said. "Well, good luck," said one of the caretakers. Your mother hates anyone to touch her hair."

But I made the appointment anyway, bundled Mom up and drove her out. It took a couple of us to help her to the chair and sink, but the results were pleasing. Mom was happy with it, too. She went back to the Home, looking quite beautiful. I went home, quite exhausted!

We had a big party for Mom's 90th birthday on our property. It was a beautiful August day. Some of her nieces came in from far away. Mom was pleased to see them, although she kept asking over and over, who they were. She couldn't remember things for very long, but everyone understood. At 90 years of age, Mom was still doing okay, and walking around with just a cane.

Some days, Mom would refuse to budge. She didn't want to go out. She just wanted to sleep. She would find all kinds of excuses of why she should stay in. Finally, I had enough of it. I pulled out her shoes and sweaters and said we were going to my house for a picnic. She protested, but consented to my prodding her into the car. She had a good time once she was settled on my back porch deck. It was Mother's Day, and it was good to have her there.

Mom was always confused, no matter where we went. "Are we going to the doctor?" she would ask. Or she would say, "Are we there yet?" Or, "why is it so far?" One Sunday we took her up the lake and carried her onto my daughter's pleasure cabin cruiser. It was tricky, hoisting her over the deep-water gulch between the deck and the boat, but we made it! We went for a long ride on Lake Michigan.

Later, we stopped at a restaurant. Mom's eating habits left something to be desired. My daughter watched as Mom stuffed spaghetti into her mouth. "Well," my daughter said, "at least she got it in." When we got Mom back to the Home after our day trip, she called out, "Don't forget to get my suitcase out of the trunk!" In her mind, she had been off on a long trip. Sometimes memory loss can be a good thing, as Mom thought she had had an adventure. Well, she had!

Some family members found Mom's table manners alarming. They didn't like to see the elderly in bibs and making a mess all over the floor with the crumbs. But our dogs liked it. They looked forward to cleaning up the dining room when Mom was done eating. When we are elderly, we don't know the things we do, and how we might offend someone else. It's just as well.

Some days, Mom would ramble. "I was busy today," she said one day. "I was on the roof." I asked what she was doing up there, but she couldn't hear me.

She talked a lot about the past. "They threw rocks at us," she said, meaning the Polish family that lived at the end of the drive that went to her Pennsylvania family home in the mining country in the hills. German and Polish families sometimes didn't get along, probably because they couldn't understand each other's language.

"Do you remember the store at the end of the drive?" she asked, and, of course, I didn't, but I was interested. "It was the Johnson Store, she went on, "and people would gather in it to visit all the time." She also told about her cousin who, while Mom was a governess in New York City working to send money home to her widowed mother and family, took back a dress Mom had just bought and brought back one that was two sizes too big. She did this, Mom said, because she was jealous of Mom's slim figure. Mom had a cute figure and was quite the dish. "Well," the cousin had said, "you didn't look good in it anyway." But of course Mom had!

In fact, Mom liked telling how an artist wanted her to pose for him and she told him she would have to ask her fiancé, who was my Dad. Dad objected and so Mom never did pose. The artist was Norman Rockwell.

She also told how she wanted to go to school in the worst way, but after the fourth grade, her mother insisted that she stay home and help with the family. "But I would run out the door and pretend I didn't hear her calling," Mom said. But after fourth grade, her mother made her drop out.

Maybe that's why Mom became such a proficient pianist. She played music that makes me flinch just looking at all the sharps and flats. All her life, she played the piano. It helped her through thick and thin and provided enjoyment for many others. While some couples sat and played cards, Mom would sit and play the piano.

It was hard to see Mom just sitting on her bed. "Is he staying with you?" she asked me when my husband and I entered her room. I winked at my husband. "Yes, I'm letting him spend the night," I said.

CHAPTER 12

All through the years, Mom kept her sense of humor. She kept people smiling with her remarks. She could be very direct. If she didn't like something, she would tell you. The grandchildren were used to gramma telling them that their "hair was too long." Their "dresses were too short." The "color was wrong." Maybe they didn't like the criticism and that's why they stopped coming, but she told it like it was. Today, when I wear black, I think of Mom, and make a mental note to get rid of the black in my wardrobe, or at least some of it.

Mom's favorite color was red. We bought her a sweet little red wool coat. She loved it. Mom was very little. By now she probably didn't weigh 90 pounds. She wore a little red hat with her coat, as well as her red gloves and little red purse. She always took her purse with her, even though there wasn't much in it. Women are like that. Purses are their sense of identity.

But it was getting harder now to get Mom in and out of places. Even though she was little, it was difficult to maneuver her here and there. At a birthday party that we were hosting outdoors, she indicated she had to go to the bathroom. We had quite a time getting her into the bathroom that was in our basement area adjacent to the party in the pole barn. When we brought her back out, she couldn't remember having been there and indicated she needed to go again. About that time, we decided that maybe it was time to take her back to the Home.

Mom had no sense of time. When we took her back to the Home, she would say, "Did someone remember to bring my suitcase?" Or she would say, "I have to get back to the Home. My husband will be waiting for me."

We received word one Christmas that Sam passed away. "Do you want us to send Sam's cremains to your mother," we were asked. "No," we quickly replied. "She wouldn't know what to do with them." It was agreed they would be brought to Michigan and placed in his family cemetery by his family members. We told Mom he died, but weren't sure she understood who he was and what happened. Mom had difficulty remembering the last thirty years. She and Sam had been married almost twenty-five years, but she had trouble remembering him.

Mom talked often about my Dad. Dad had died suddenly at age 57 from cancer of the liver. He was diagnosed and died within a span of six weeks. Dad had been the love of Mom's life, and she talked frequently about him. She and Sam, all in all, had had a good relationship too. It was just that she couldn't deal with taking care of someone in her later years. It was too much. She would have had the same problem with my Dad.

She tired easily now. She didn't have an interest in walking down to the meadow anymore. We took her for rides and let her sit on the park bench beside the river. We ate ice cream from Dixie cups and watched the ducks and fishermen.

"Tochter," she would say, "Where are their wives?" she asked, watching two fishermen getting into a boat. "It's sad they don't have wives." To Mom, everyone had to have a wife. A wife, to Mom's way of thinking, was supposed to always be by her husband's side.

I was feeling sad knowing that the day would come when I wouldn't have anyone call me "Tochter," which is German for daughter. I didn't want to think about it.

Mom's tolerance was getting low. "I have to go potty now," Mom would say, while we were in the car on our way somewhere. "Well, we are almost home," I would lie, and hope that we got there before it was too late. "But I have to go now," she would repeat, and my husband stepped on the accelerator a little harder.

She slept more and more. It was an effort to wake her for visits. She would sit up for a minute or two and then flop back down on the bed. It was a bigger effort to bring her to our homes. She had several little mini-strokes. Her skin was tissue thin and easily blotched with red patches.

The Christmas of her 91st year, my husband went to pick her up at the home. She had had a bad night and didn't seem to be with it at all. Apparently she had had another little mini stroke. The caretakers placed her in a wheelchair. Laboriously, she was maneuvered over to our house.

She sat quietly. Her speech was slurred. She didn't want to stay long. She missed her husband. After awhile we took her home.

She had several hospital visits after that and used the wheelchair frequently. I hated to send her to the hospital and watch her get plugged in to all the devices. It seemed so inhumane, especially to the elderly. Mom's veins were thin and prominent. I winced along with her when she needed to have IV's.

One Christmas I was in charge of the annual tree lighting festival at out town, but the Home called, and I ended up taking Mom to the hospital instead. She looked so pathetic. We knew someday one of the visits would be a last one. "Is this your mother?" an aide said. The aide was helping push Mom's wheelchair towards our car. "Yes," I said. "Bless you," said the aide. She could see that we were having a difficult time.

Mom would protest at the least little thing. She cried when we put on her coat, and complained when we pulled on her mittens. She had a hard time getting into and out of the car. But we didn't want her to stagnate. We felt we had to keep her moving.

"She won't let us do anything for her," the workers would complain. "When we dress her for bed, she gets up and changes her clothes." We didn't know what to do or say.

"I want to go," she would say. "I want to cross over to the other side." She didn't like the situation she found herself in. It was hard to watch her decline. We hoped she wasn't in pain. She had a problem, for a while with peanuts and chocolate. Her system couldn't handle them. We had to make sure she didn't get any. She didn't care about the wine anymore. She didn't care about much of anything anymore, other than sleeping.

My sister and I would visit the home and play the piano. There was a time when Mom would be critical of my playing, but not anymore. But sometimes she never came out of her room to listen. She just wanted to sleep. Her room didn't smell very nice. We sprayed it with cologne.

We dreaded going to the Home to watch her lie on her bed and look so pathetic. Her needs were becoming more dramatic. "Do you think she needs to go in a nursing home?" we asked, watching the caregivers in their distress over caring for her. "No," they said, "she has been here for several years. We want her to stay here until the end." We thanked them and silently applauded their determination and courage.

Mom had her spell about things. There was a time when she insisted someone stole the clock from her dresser. We couldn't imagine what clock she meant, as there hadn't been a clock there, that we could recall, but I found a cute little one with pink rosebuds on it, and put it on her night stand one day, and we never heard a word again about the stolen clock.

"They leave it here to threaten me," she said. "What, Mom?" I asked. "The jacket. See that white jacket over there? It belongs to those boys who left it here as a threat." I looked at the jacket. It was one I had bought for her once at a garage sale. "I'll take it with me," I said, draping the offending jacket over my arm. I didn't know at the time that dementia does that. It plays tricks with the mind in various ways.

"My husband gave me this," Mom said one day, fingering the necklace around her neck, "and I can't get it off." I chuckled as I removed it. It was a necklace she had been given as a gift. I had wondered, at the time, if Mom would be able to get it off herself. Apparently not.

"Did you take what I had for you?" asked Mom as I headed for the door. Mom had always insisted on giving us something when she was in her own home. That brought back memories when we visited several aunts in another town. We never left their homes, either, without a sweet kucken or a bag of cookies. Mom was that way. No one left her house empty handed. Maybe it was part of the warm German hospitality.

CHAPTER 13

Christmas of Mom's 92nd year was a pleasant one. Mom seemed content, at least for a while. She had color in her cheeks. She used a walker most of the time now. But she had no patience. "I need to get back to my home," she said after awhile. "My husband will be waiting." It was a good, but short, visit.

I brought nail polish with me to the Home and painted Mom's nails. When I cut them, Mom complained and said they didn't need cutting. She would howl even before I got out the scissors, but I clenched my teeth and went ahead and did it. I looked forward to doing her nails. She always wore a necklace, too, and earrings.

"Where are your rings?" I asked one day when I noticed that her fingers were bare. "Oh," she said, "I put them away in a box." I cringed at the remark. Mom had stuff stashed all over her room. I wondered if we would ever find them.

The red blotches on Mom's ankles were getting worse. When one seemed to pop, we had to take her to the doctor and then to the specialist. "We might have to do a skin graft," the specialist said. "Whose skin will you graft, doctor," I asked. Mom's skin was tissue paper thin all over. "Hmm," he said, "you have a good point." He didn't mention grafting after that.

The infection had worsened when a medication that was placed on it contained sulfa. Mom was allergic to sulfa. We had told people that, but somehow no one noticed that the medication they put on it contained sulfa. Somehow, we hadn't caught that either. One has to be so careful and alert. But in this instance we were applying medication that was doing more harm than good. We thought we were watching everything, but sometimes we missed something important. Sometimes we trusted others too much.

I read in a medical book that some heart medicine might cause red blotches. "Maybe," said the doctor reluctantly, "we need to change the medication," when I told him of my suspicions.

We hadn't taken Mom out much that winter. She hated the cold. She tired easily and was difficult to move. She just wanted to sleep. "I want to go home," she would say.

The weather was rainy and cold all spring. We were waiting for nice weather so we could take her out.

None of us were getting any younger. We discussed the possibility that Mom might outlive us. Maybe we should continue with our own lives. We started mentally letting "Mom go." Maybe we had been holding on to her too tightly.

When one of us went on trips, we made sure one of us stayed home, just in case. We wondered what we would do if something happened while we were away. A manager of a cruise line we were looking into, said she told her family to "put her mom on ice, if something happened" while she was gone. That seemed a little harsh, and yet one does have to face reality that things sometimes happen at the most inopportune times.

One afternoon at the Home we were sitting and visiting. Mom had tried to play the piano, but just couldn't get it together. A family came to visit with another resident. Mom tried to disrupt their visit. I tried to discourage her. "You wouldn't let me talk with them," Mom scolded after they left. "I was going to ask them for a ride home!"

Mom always knew who we were, but she had a hard time remembering the grandchildren, since they didn't often visit. But she always knew who I was, as well as my sister. We realized she was driving the residents crazy by asking them over and over again, for their names, day after day, hour after hour. She annoyed some of the residents. We could hear some of them mumble, "shut up" to her, but she couldn't hear them. We were glad her hearing was impaired so she couldn't hear the daily insults.

Nor did some of the residents like her playing the piano. They would bang on the wall or close their doors or leave the room in a scowl. The piano disrupted their television time. Mom wasn't interested in television, and played the piano anyway. Our stomachs would turn when we would see the little "situations" occur that we couldn't control. It didn't seem to bother Mom. Maybe it bothered us more than it did her.

We marveled at the patience of the workers. It takes a saintly person to work with the elderly. We wondered if anyone would be as patient with us when we get to that time in life.

In June, Mom seemed to be doing okay. We visited with her on a Saturday. When she walked down the hall with me, she asked, "Where is my accordion?" "Mom," I said, "Remember, I took it home and it's in my attic." "Your attic," she said indignantly, "I need it here so I can play it." Mom had taken accordion lessons and at one time owned one of the grand size accordions. She sold it a few years ago and now owned an average sized one. She was quite good on it, although the grandchildren didn't like it. "It's too noisy," they would say. But maybe that's because Mom insisted on having it plugged in to an amplifier!

On Monday morning, the telephone rang. "Come quickly" said the caller. "Your Mom is not breathing right. I have called 9-1-1." How can that be, I thought. She seemed okay on Saturday. I started grabbing my purse and things. If this meant a visit to the hospital, I wanted to take along a candy bar and sewing, as that usually meant an all day stay.

The phone rang again. "Bring your Mom's medical papers," the voice continued. "I think your Mom is taking her last breath." I called my sister and we leaped into action. When we arrived at the Home, the paramedics were there. "Do you have the medical forms?" they asked as soon as I entered the hall. I could see Mom stretched out on the floor. "She's gone," said the caretaker. "Mary died," said the caretaker's two year old little granddaughter who had been spending the night at the Home.

With shaking fingers I pulled out the medical forms. Through my blurry eyes, I couldn't tell what was what. "Here," I said, handing the stack of forms to the paramedic. "Do you want her on life support?" The Big Question. I knew Mom didn't want life support.

After the paramedics and deputies left, we were allowed to go in Mom's room and say goodbye. We told her we loved her and thanked her for being a good mother. I noticed her nails needed to be clipped and polished. I was going to do that tomorrow. Why hadn't I done that on Saturday, I asked myself?

We watched as the hearse pulled out of the driveway. Mom had gone home.

CHAPTER 14

When we searched Mom's room, later that evening, we found her rings and had them placed on her fingers. Of all places, they were in her jewelry box! We marveled that Mom had moved on to the next world without pain. "A Shone Totte," said my cousin, which meant "A good death." Mom had been at the Home for six years. In her second year at the Home, we had made funeral arrangements. We weren't sure what might be ahead of us and we wanted to be sure there was money set aside for the funeral. We had purchased a beautiful lavender dress for Mom, as well.

That was a good decision, as, when the time came, we had enough to do without going through all the other things. It's best to make such decisions when one isn't under emotional duress. There were people to call. Services to be arranged. We felt numb and drained. Even though we knew this day would come, it was still a shock.

Later, the caretakers at the Home told us amusing stories about Mom. They told how she came out of her room once, using her bra for a belt. Another time she asked a resident who had just lost his wife, if he "had found another bed mate yet." Her funeral was a "Celebration of Life." At the graveside we sang, "When the roll is called up yonder, I'll be there." It seemed a fitting tribute to Mom.

Mom had a way of making others happy despite her own misery and discomfort in her final years. She had lived a good life, an adventurous life. She had crossed the Atlantic from Germany on the White Star Line. Her family had attempted to book passage on the Titanic, but it was full. Mom told us that she remembered, when two weeks later they passed the last known area of the Titanic, seeing bodies and debris floating in the water. Mom had only been four and a half years old at the time, traveling with her mother, baby brother, and older sister.

Mother had seen a lot. She lived through two world wars. She had seen civilization go from horse and buggies to automobiles. She survived through the Big Depression. She lived during the days of kerosene lamps and outhouses. She worked in New York City as a governess. She attended a little German Lutheran Church in Winburne, Pennsylvania where her father was the choirmaster and her mother taught Sunday school. She was the next oldest of nine children. When she passed on, only her younger brother survived, but he, too, made his journey before the year was up.

Mother lived during the era when most mothers stayed home with their families, as opposed to working in the outside world. But how could mothers work in those days when everything from clothes washing to baking had to be done laboriously by hand? Clothes had to be sewn. Bread had to be baked. Mother, like a lot of women, canned everything she could get her hands on, from wild huckleberries and chokecherries to veal and tomatoes.

When we needed to go into town and Dad was at work, we hitchhiked a ride on the main road. Since we knew most of the people who might be driving, it wasn't a risk.

Dad came over from Germany when he was nineteen. His aunt had sponsored him. Both he and Mom remembered going through Ellis Island. Unfortunately, they never talked about it much, so I was never able to hear about their experiences. Of course, Mom had been quite young, but Dad, surely would have had things to tell. We never think to ask our parents about their growing up days or early experiences, until it is too late. Today I would love to hear their stories.

When we lived in the mountains, women visited one another during the week days. How enjoyable those visits were! As a family we went to the movies, or Mom and I would go to bingo on Wednesday nights. Family was so important.

We had so many wonderful picnics at the little creek in the mountain. We would spread our tablecloth on the big boulder protruding into the creek, and surrounded by laurel bush and hemlock, we ate the wonderful food that Mom always packed. Both Mom and Dad liked picnics. Mom baked wonderful cream pies and sometimes by the time we got to the lake, the pie would be pudding. But secretly, I loved those runny cream pies.

We were always visiting someone, and we enjoyed our aunts, uncles and cousins, until one by one, some of them started moving off to the cities.

Electricity was not available for many years at our little bungalow that Dad built in the valley. One time the kerosene lamp fell over and Dad's chair was ablaze. Many homes burned down due to kerosene lamps and overheated coal furnaces. When I was very small, Mom clipped little candles on our Christmas tree. It's a wonder the tree never caught on fire. But it didn't.

Dad loved Christmas so much. He did his own Christmas shopping and would wrap his presents for us in white tissue paper. He loved to shop for his "three women." I remember the year we went to an adjacent town and Dad picked out a beautiful velvet bathrobe fore Mom. It was the most beautiful robe I had ever seen. I can still visualize it, deep green velvet and decorated with deep primroses. Dad was always buying special things for his girls: Mom, my sister, and me.

One Christmas Dad gave each of us a necklace of wooden beads. Mine was bright red. My sister's was green, and Mother's was blue. I always treasured those little beads.

Even the telephone wasn't available during my early childhood. I remember when the lines were brought down our long driveway to our house. We were all afraid to answer the phone when it was first installed. Every house was assigned a certain number of rings. You answered the phone when you heard your number of rings. People listened in on other people's conversations. If there was an emergency, you would tell the other people to get off the line.

If the telephone rang in the middle of the night, you knew someone died. That's just the way it was. Everyone knew what was going on.

Our water came from a reservoir that Dad built at the foot of the hill. It ran by gravity. In the wintertime we would hear Dad downstairs banging on the pipes when they got frozen up.

Our house was heated by coal. The fire would often go out during the night, and we huddled under our blankets. There was one large register in the middle of the hall. It was a great place to spread our underwear to warm up. How toasty it felt to pull on those warm clothes. But I did worry about the fiery red-hot furnace that looked like a monster!

No one had storm windows. The wind would blow and bang the windows so much that Mom would get up and stuff rags in them.

We had a separate little stove for the water heater. All of us had to keep it fueled with coal. If we didn't, we wouldn't have any hot water. Before we had indoor plumbing, we had to go outside to the outhouse that was far out back beyond the chicken coop. We kept it supplied with catalogues, for tissue. I remember how cold it was at nighttime.

On our twenty acres we kept a cow and chickens. It was my job to keep the mother hens from taking their little chicks into the woods where the skunk and fox would catch them. Sometimes I didn't succeed, and the flock would be diminished. Mom would milk the cow and strain the cream from the milk. Many times we had fresh whipped cream for our cocoa. We churned our own butter, and Mom baked our own bread. We ate a lot of chicken, and Mom used the feathers for stuffing pillows. It was quite a job, steaming those chickens so the feathers could be plucked.

During World War II, there was a rationing of goods and material. We couldn't visit as much as we wanted to as we received coupons that allowed only enough gas for Dad to drive to work. Because we had a small family, we received a very limited number of coupons for sugar and flour. Mom would take some of our outgrown coats to one of the big farm families on the other side of the mountain, in exchange for sugar and flour coupons.

Mom and Dad both belonged to the Grange organization. The Grange was a fraternal order to help the farming community. I well remember the wonderful suppers from all the delicious foods the farm families brought to the Grange meetings. We worked together to prepare booths for the Grange and for our local 4-H, in the local county fair every summer. We participated in skits and plays that were performed for our own and visiting Granges. We traveled to other towns and states to be initiated into the various "degrees" of Grange. We all earned the highest degree, the seventh, in the Grange organization.

Dad belonged to the National Guard and went off to guard camp at Indian Town Gap every summer. He would be gone for two weeks, but when he came home, he brought special presents for all of us. He was too old to be in World War II, but did his duty by participating in the Guards. I looked forward to the postcards he would send from camp. We went to the National Armory in town for family night, and it was there that Dad taught me how to dance the polka.

We picked huckleberries and blackberries by the bushel, up in the mountains. Wild chestnuts grew on bushes along the old abandoned county road that ran along the side of our house. We swam in the creek by the house and enjoyed life in the country until the coal mine industry died, and the mines closed down.

Dad allowed a local company to strip-mine our hill for coal. We were saddened to see the coal trucks come roaring down the road. Dad never received the amount of money he thought he would receive from that venture. The mining resulted in the loss of our water system on the hill, and greatly disfigured the mountainsides that we all loved so much. But in those days the owner of land did not own the mineral rights.

Dad studied to be a mining inspector, but times were changing. The coal mines were closing down, one by one. Dad went off to the big cities, seeking work. For a while he went to Cleveland where I once took the bus to visit him. Together we rode the train to the beach. He was so excited about our little trip together. But when we got there, the beach was polluted, and had a big "Closed" sign on it, and we had to go back to his apartment. Dad was so disappointed.

Finally, our family decided to follow some of our aunts and uncles who had moved to the Michigan area. Dad left Cleveland and found a job in Michigan. We packed up and away we moved. It was my junior year in high school. I really didn't want to move, but there was no choice.

Dad missed the mountains. We all did. That's when Mom began taking formal piano lessons. She took adversity and turned it into opportunity. Dad passed away six years after our move. I think he never truly adjusted to city life. He had to work in a situation that necessitated strong fumes. We think that experience shortened his life.

When my husband and I went to Halifax one recent spring, we were told that Titanic debris was, indeed, on the surface several weeks after the ship sank, which confirmed what Mom saw when she was a little girl. We were glad Mom's family had been turned away and had to book a different liner. Otherwise, I would not have this story to share.

POSTSCRIPT

Every state seems to have a different set of rules for homes for the elderly. It is important to contact your own state to find out what they have to offer. Housing for the elderly includes assisted living facilities, nursing homes, foster care homes, personnel living homes, retirement homes, to name a few. Things to consider, when looking at facilities are as follows: Are bedrooms one bed or two? Mom had a private room with a bed, her dresser and chair. She was probably the only resident who did not want a telephone, television, or radio in her room. A private bathroom is important. In Mom's case, a porta potty was in the closet. That seemed to suit her just fine.

That's one thing to look for—those porta potties—make sure they get emptied on a timely basis! Is the Home clean and neat? We looked at a wide range of elderly homes. Some were absolutely dreadful!

How safe is the neighborhood? The home we placed Mom in was in the country, with rolling fields and pleasant scenery, because that was the environment to which she was accustomed. It's important to check references, to make certain the caretakers are reliable and honest.

Is there adequate help? How many people are on duty? Does the kitchen area look sanitary and safe? Do they have responsible staff that sleeps overnight? What activities are offered? Mom greatly enjoyed the "Music Man" that came once a week. He played music and challenged their brains with questions. Is the Home visited by organizations such as the Girl Scouts, school groups, etc.? It's important that children visit once in a while. What about religious services? Are they offered? What other activities take place?

What medical services are available? At Mom's Home a foot doctor made monthly inspections. What about hair care? Mom enjoyed her visits "out" to the hairdresser until her last year. Eventually, a hairdresser started coming to give haircuts and permanents on a regular basis. Do the residents look healthy and happy? How is the food? Is the driveway cleared in winter? Is there a porch, deck, garden and/or flowerbeds? All of these things make a Home enjoyable.

What about cost? In Mom's case, she paid her own way through social security and her own savings.

How large is the facility? Does it hold ten, twelve or more? Does the facility cater only to the elderly or are there also mentally challenged persons? Safety is a big concern. Does the facility house just women? Mother enjoyed male companionship just as much as female companionship.

The above are just some of the questions one needs to assess when looking at placing an elderly parent or other relative. When we began looking at facilities, we were quite disturbed in the difference in them. Some did not look safe, or were dark and drab. One even had "honey buckets" by the bedsides! Another was in a bad neighborhood. One accepted mental patients as well as elderly. We wanted as cozy an environment possible, for our Mother. We did not want our Mother in a "hospital style" home. As it was, Mom was happy in her little room in Maplewood. She considered Maplewood her home.

All of the above needs to be taken into consideration. After all, our loved ones deserve only the best of care, the best there is to offer.

Printed in the United States
By Bookmasters